Ultimate Le
Superhumaı

Learning

Brain Training And Plasticity Techniques For Memory Improvement, Productivity, Speed Reading, And To Increase Your Learning Speed!

Ryan Cooper

STOP!!! Before you read any further....Would you like to know the Success Secrets of how to make Passive Income Online?

If your answer is yes, then you are not alone. Thousands of people are looking for the secret to learning how to create their own online passive income style business.

If you have been searching for these answers without much luck, you are in the right place!

Because I want to make sure to give you as much value as possible for purchasing this book, right now for a limited time you can get 3 incredible bonuses for free.

At the end of this book I describe all 3 bonuses. You can access them at the end. But for those of you that want to grab your bonuses right now. See below.

Just Go Here For Free Instant Access:

www.OperationAwesomeLife.com/FreeBonuses

Legal Notice

Disclaimer Notice

Table Of Contents

Introduction

I want to thank you and congratulate you for purchasing the book, *"Learning: Ultimate Learning Superhuman Guide! -Brain Training And Plasticity Techniques For Memory Improvement, Productivity, Speed Reading, And To Increase Your Learning Speed!"*.

This "Learning" book contains proven steps and strategies on how to use the natural capabilities of the human brain when it comes to achieving better learning outcomes. Some research revealed that the human brain actually possesses the power to surpass learning standards that we have set in the past. We need to understand it better in order to really tap into its full potential.

Training the brain is possible. However, there are right and wrong ways of doing it. You must be on the right track if you really don't want your effort and time to be wasted on brain training. The concepts and methods of brain training, memory improvement, speed reading, and super-fast learning as presented on this book should lead you into the right direction.

Make no mistake about it as there is no such thing as instant positive results. What you will learn from this book are tools that you can use to produce gradual and consistent positive learning outcomes. While it might take time to apply the things you will learn here, a little patience will guarantee that everything will pay off in the end.

Are you ready to become a "super learner"? If your answer is yes, then this is the perfect book for you to read!

Thanks again for purchasing this book, I hope you enjoy it!

Chapter 1: Introduction To Super Learning

The concept of super learning is quite controversial these days. The need to learn fast and with great efficiency is something that has been brought by the current developments in our society. Everything has been hyped up and this means that members of this generation need to exert a lot of effort in order to catch up. Since researches have revealed that the human brain has really great capacity for learning, there are efforts to push over its boundaries.

This is where the concept and system of super learning was formed. Now, what really is this "super learning" system that we commonly see online these days? By definition, it is the fastest way to learn things using a combination of conventional and nonconventional methods. Yes, it harnesses the brain's natural capability known as plasticity in order to maximize learning outcomes even under unfavorable conditions.

Is super learning relevant for us these days? Yes, and this is because of the current pace at which technological advancements are taking over society. Social media applications, multiple intelligence based education programs, distance education and curriculum innovations are being seen. An individual needs a way to really catch up with these things in order to adapt well and thrive in this modern world.

While super learning seems easy to do, there are challenges that one will encounter which will make the task of a learner quite complicated. First of all, the concept of super learning is not really taught in schools. Next, only a few educators have really trained to teach the concepts of super learning. Aside from this, there are also many forms of literature about unconventional methods of learning that are available these days. Confusions could easily arise under such situations.

It is very obvious that there are lots of programs that are supposed to boost the learning capacities of individuals. One should just choose which one to use for specific needs. Have you ever heard about Quantum Super Learning Tech, Master Mind, and Super Memory? These systems are based on the principles of super learning as a whole.

To be able to understand the concept of super learning, there are things that you must expect about it. One is all about the steps that are involved in the system. These steps include the following:

- Proper brain preparation.
- Immersion in diverse forms of learning materials.
- Use of conventional and unconventional learning techniques.
- Processing and storage of acquired information or new learning.
- Revision of acquired information/learning for maximum benefits.
- Application of learning.

It is important too that you have realistic sets of expectations about super learning. These are as follows:

1. *Everything will be time-bound*: There is a time frame for the process as well as for the manifestation of results.
2. *Results will get manifested progressively*: There is no such thing as instant or overnight positive results when it comes to super learning. It is impossible to learn the contents of an entire book within a single session. However, it is possible to fast track the learning progress through regular short sessions.
3. *Super learning is intensity-based*: If faster and higher qualities of results need to be achieved, the intensity of activities could be increased. Of course, this means that you can go as fast or as slow as you wish through the process.

Now that you have been properly introduced to the basics of super learning, it is time to start your quest on acquiring its ways, techniques and applications. The next chapter will set you on the right track.

Chapter 2: Breaking Old Habits

Super learning as a new system deviates from the traditional ways of education. Its concepts and benefits become hard to grasp because of old habits that might have formed within an individual as a result of the previous systems of learning used. If you are aiming to make the most out of what the super learning system has to offer, then you need to be open to changes. It means letting go of old habits and forming new ones as needed. These new habits are suited to the methodologies within the super learning system.

Are you aware of what habits you might have now that have significant amounts of impact on how fast you learn? Look at the following and see if there are familiar things that you'll recognize:

- Studying while in bed.
- Eating while studying.
- Procrastinating or postponing tasks even when deadlines are obviously around the corner.
- Studying while in front of a PC and Facebook (and/or other social media accounts) is open in the tab.
- Cramming during times of examination.
- Waking up late.
- Not taking notes during lectures in anticipation that a handout will be distributed later.

If you see yourself guilty of any of the things mentioned above, it means that you are not yet ready for the super learning system. There is a need to identify and conquer bad habits and to form new positive ones. These new habits will pave the way to the effectiveness of super learning techniques that will be used.

There is no need to complicate the whole habit modification task. By understanding the cycle of habit formation, you can easily have your way around this task. The cycle is composed of the following stages:

1. TRIGGER – Any signal that tells your brain to show the habit in an automatic manner (unconscious action).
2. ROUTINE – This is the actual habit or behavior. Its continuous manifestation once it shows up will depend upon the level of control that an individual will have over it.
3. INCENTIVE – An action or material that would lead the brain to remember and repeat the routine in the future. As long as the brain feels that it has been "rewarded", the routine will have a stronger reinforcement within the memory and will be repeated easily once the trigger appears.

Cutting through any of these processes or stages of habit formation would allow an individual to learn and "unlearn" things. Knowledge about this cycle is very useful if you want to take control of your habits by breaking the old (bad) and forming new ones (good). The role of the environment is also crucial in the process. Automatic behavior tends to be repeated if there will be no change in the environment where an individual stays. This explains why rehabilitation facilities are so effective in breaking the toughest bad habits (addiction).

Considering the concept above, the following tips should help you break old habits without struggling much:

- **Focus on one habit before going on to another**: Success rate will be higher if this course of action is taken. Multi-tasking in breaking old habits will just lead to the creation of additional unwanted routines.
- **Create a signal that will really catch your attention**: The more bizarre your signal is, the more effective it will be. If you find yourself not responding to the usual sound of the alarm clock, then connect it to a speaker. This way, you'll definitely be jumping out of bed on the designated time.
- **Compensate for the benefits you think you are getting from the old habit**: We don't just pull out habits. They are there for a reason and this is because there are needs that are solved. If you are associating your tardiness to lack of sleep each night, go to bed earlier than usual or take power naps (5-15 minutes) within the day.

- **<u>Evaluate the results of your efforts</u>**: It should show you that there is balance between sacrifices and gains. If it pains you to stick to the new habit and you see that it isn't really working, let it go.
- **<u>Flood bad thoughts with positivity</u>**: If you find yourself getting negative about a situation, come up with thoughts that highlight some positive things you are getting. When you are always turning off your phone when studying for an hour and you feel disconnected with the rest of the world, think about how your grades are improving.
- **<u>Be consistent</u>**: Repeating the new habit to be formed trains the brain to retain it and automatically manifest it upon the appearance of a signal. Regularity of reinforcement ensures success in new habit formation.

Chapter 3: The Power Of Mind Mapping

It is said that when you take notes, you also learn. By elevating note taking through the use of creatively designed visual cues, another very important tool in learning is produced. Yes, we are talking about mind mapping. Basically, mind mapping is the process of capturing one's thoughts and transforming them into something visual. The creation of mind maps is a very basic skill that needs no complicated pre-requisite training.

If we will look at it, these mind maps are diagrams that start out from a center object or subject and branches out into sub-topics. A fully constructed mind map looks like a tree with a central branch from which various ideas stem out. The thing that makes a mind map's elements unique is that each could be connected and gives out related ideas.

There are many applications for mind maps. The following are just some of the most relevant:

- Taking up a course or subject.
- Career planning and evaluation of decisions to be made.
- Creation of review or learning materials that can be compiled in an online or physical knowledge bank (file folders).
- Problem solving on any subject or scenario.
- Summary generation (for book reports).
- Cooperative learning scenarios or team presentations.

Yes, mind mapping is often compared to ordinary note taking procedure. However, those who do this will often end up with a realization that mind mapping is more important when a super learning scenario is present. There are many reasons why this system of organizing thoughts and information is so effective.

The first one is that it boosts up the capacity of the brain to remember. If we will recall, the brain works best by associating images and words when it is trying to learn. Mind mapping uses symbols, pictures, colors, numbers and texts when organizing information. Compare this with note taking which only uses written words to organize and present information. Current researchers have discovered that mind mapping is six times more effective than note taking when it comes to developing memory.

Next, mind mapping allows an individual like you to easily associate information with other sets of information based on common grounds. This is a great way to exercise the mind while coming up with a tangible output for review. Through associations, it is easy to see what things are still missing in the diagram. Full elaboration of a topic is therefore done even when you think you can't do it.

A broad topic can easily be understood through mind mapping. A mind map gives an individual a full view of the coverage of a topic or subject. It allows us to see our progress when we are trying to cover the subtopics of an entire course or a chapter. Even if there are only a handful of symbols on the map, it could hold and represent huge amounts of information. This is what makes such maps convenient and effective to use for those who want to review or study out of normal classroom or study session setting.

By using mind mapping, you will have the capability to work faster through a learning task. Juggling complicated learning concepts is possible even if there is limited time allocated for the whole thing. The use of mind mapping is very much observed within institutions of higher education (colleges and universities). Of course, its use in the corporate world is very obvious now too. Executives and administrators use this technique or system during planning sessions, meetings, and seminars.

The power of mind mapping in helping individuals learn faster cannot be underestimated. It is a skill that is worth learning and using no matter if you are within or outside an academic environment. Now, mind mapping is just one of the many components of super learning. There are still many elements that you should take a look at and start getting familiar with. The next chapter tackles another important tool in the super learning process: your memory. Go on and read more!

Chapter 4: Tricks And Tips For Improving Your Memory

Learning and memory are linked to each other. It is necessary to build and boost the capability of your memory first before making any attempt to get involved in super learning tasks. It is common for us to think that memory improvement is an easy thing to do. In fact, people will readily assume that if they will review a learning material for long periods of time, their memory will get better. Some will even resort to taking in "memory enhancing pills" to fast track their progress.

Improving your memory can turn out to be eithera complicated or an easy thing to do. Do the process wrong and you will end up with bad learning habits. If you will do it through the recommended and research-backed methods, you will be one step closer to being a "super learner".

Basically, there are two types of memory that all of us have. Yes, these include short and long term memories. Short term memory is useful when you need to remember bits of information on the spot. A plate number, the name of the girl introduced to you, and even the number combination on your new lock can be remembered through short term memory. Long-term memory is used for learning tasks that require you to store large amounts of information that need to be used later. The information on a whole chapter of a book that will be used for an exam a week from now requires long-term memory.

The following tips and tricks should get your memory improved for fast or super learning tasks:

- **_Feed your brain_**: The center of all of your memory ability is your brain. Supplement it with nutrients that help boost its capability to transmit neural impulses fast. Food items that are known sources of Omega-3 and basic amino acids are recommended. Yes, there are memory-enhancing pills available in the market, but their effects are often short-lived. There are also reports of memory decline among those who have continuously used these supplements and suddenly stopped. It will be better to stick to natural sources of memory-boosting nutrients like oily fish, blueberries, tomatoes, blackcurrant, pumpkin seeds, sage, broccoli and nuts.

- *__Dump multi-tasking when doing learning tasks__*. The key here is to focus on one task at a time. Multi-tasking is good only when you already have a higher level of memory that has been developed through many years of training. By focusing on one learning task at a time, you increase your brain's capability to absorb more information.
- *__Use as many senses as possible when memorizing things__*: This explains why those who recite what they read and touch remember more. If you can use your eyes, hands, nose, and ears while trying to memorize something, the chances of information retention are higher. This might not work in speed reading where you are trying to aim for both quantity of information and comprehension. However, for recalling data, this trick works well enough.
- *__Overlearning something by repeating it__*: The repetition action forces your brain to remember a set of information. This is effective, once again, if you are just aiming for simple recall of facts and not for comprehension. A lot of people know how this technique works, but they tend to rely mostly on it even if their purpose doesn't match its true use.
- *__Explore a memorization style that works for you__*: Modern educational psychologists now use the multiple intelligence concepts when they are trying to explain different learning styles. You should explore which one works best for you. If you will find one style that suits your abilities and interests, then stick to it. If you find listening to music helpful when you memorize, then use this technique whenever you are reviewing.
- *__Proceed with learning tasks when your mind and body has rested enough__*: If there are people who claim that studying during the early hours of the morning helped them memorize faster, then this is due to the fact that they

have rested adequately. Get enough sleep by going to bed early. Wake up early and proceed with your study sessions and see how it would benefit you.

There are still many tips and tricks that you can use when you want to boost your memory. However, it is up to you to determine which ones will really match your abilities and needs. The tips mentioned above should get you started on the right track. There are websites that could offer more information about this matter. Always do your research as there are innovations and breakthroughs in memory improvement that are being published on a regular basis in the internet.

Chapter 5: Speed Reading Techniques For Beginners

Reading is one of our primary ways of acquiring new information. Learning is based on the amount of information that is acquired by the brain. The efficiency of learning is affected by the ratio between retained and forgotten information that has been visually acquired. To keep efficiency levels up, maximum amount of information acquisition must be aimed for. Such a thing is possible through speed reading.

Just like in typing on a PC keyboard, reading speed can be measured. Yes, the measurement is also in terms of WPM or words per minute. An average person can read from 200 to 300 WPM with a comprehension level of 50-60% only. There are systems or programs that claim to be able to boost reading speeds towards 300, 600, and 1000 WPM levels.

If you are aiming to be a "super learner", then there is no need to immediately attain the "thousand level" capability. The real need is focused on your ability to improve your current reading speed. You must learn the method to continuously progress through higher levels as you work.

The principles and techniques of speed-reading, if followed properly, can be a great way to improve your ability to become an independent learner. Basically, speed reading is defined as the method of acquiring information by quickly skimming or glancing through a line or group of words. There are three obstacles to speed reading. These are as follows:

- The tendency to fixate on a single word or group of word per line at an extended period of time.
- Regression or reading back which is common as a habit for many people.
- Peripheral vision use which not all people are commonly trained to use.

Taking in consideration the obstacles mentioned above, the following speed reading techniques should be helpful for a beginner:

1. **_Hold the material at a correct angle_**: A 30-degree angle is most recommended by experts. It is never a wise practice to read a learning material that is lying flat on a surface. Reading while lying on the bed is also a bad practice that should be avoided.

2. **_Eye Exercise should become a pre-reading routine_**: This involves the use of a wall which is at least 10 feet away from you. Focus your eye on the wall and using your finger, draw an infinity symbol in the air (left to right motion). Follow the pattern with your eyes only. Repeat the process by going in the opposite direction.

3. **_Move your head as you move from one line to another_**: While this practice may seem unconventional, there are research evidences that reveal that this can boost reading speed from 200 to a thousand WPM. It helps in reducing strain to the eyes and widens the range of peripheral vision.

4. **_Use a pointer when going through lines_**: A pencil or your index finger can be used for this technique. Guide your vision towards the end of the line as you read. Increase or decrease the hovering speed of your pointer over the lines as needed. This is a good technique to use when you are trying to build up your power of concentration and reduce fixation time.

5. **_Read silently_**: Vocalizing the words or lines that you read reduces your speed and comprehension. In speed reading, vocalization of words is just a distraction.

6. **_Prefer "chunk reading" over "word-for-word reading"_**: Instead of focusing on the meaning of individual words, you can aim for groups or chunks of words. In advanced levels, you can focus on internalizing entire lines of text.

7. **_Read without going back_**: This is even if you feel that you have missed ideas on the previous lines. This develops your speed. While comprehension will obviously suffer at first, it will eventually improve as your speed levels go up.

Speed-reading is a very important skill most especially for those who have needs for fast learning. Even if you are a complete beginner, you can train to speed-read on your own. With this being said, it is time to move on to brain training. The next chapter will have it covered for you.

Chapter 6: The Importance Of Brain Training

The human brain is always being compared to muscles. It needs to be trained in order to develop well. Neurologists are also using the evolutionary theory of "Use and Disuse" to explain what would happen if the brain or its parts are not kept active or used regularly. Yes, we have tendencies to have dominant use of only one specific hemisphere of the brain. This leads to an "imbalanced" brain in terms of function efficiency. In a learning scenario, an ideal type of brain is the one that has equal efficiency in all of its parts. Ideal brains are developed through training.

There are misconceptions about brain training at the current times. The biggest one is that it is thought of as mere tutoring. Many of us would want to undergo through such trainings because we want to be able to enumerate information, perform better in computations, or ace an upcoming test. To correct this incorrect notion about brain training, it is actually a process wherein the brain is made much stronger so that it can learn whenever there are learning tasks around.

Brain training develops an individual's power of thinking. Skills such as reasoning, imagery processing, attention, memory retention and use, and logical-spatial are improved. If we will look at some of the training programs out there that are designed to train the brain, there are strong similarities. There are activities that are designed to look and feel like games. These are progressing from easy towards more complicated and difficult levels.

So, is this training really important? If we will examine the perspective of both academically struggling and excelling individuals, its importance cannot be just undermined. For those who are having difficulties in academics, brain training teaches them to identify strengths and weaknesses. Areas of weaknesses are focused on so that learning can still happen even under unfavorable conditions.

For academically gifted or talented individuals, a brain training course or session acts as a way to solidify their skills and strengths. It also teaches them how to adapt to changes in the environment or academic setting they could possibly get exposed to. Because it is inside a human body that age up and are affected by external factors, the brain will not always function at optimal levels.

The point of training is to equip an individual with useful knowledge on how to keep the brain functioning at desirable levels. Memory reduction as one ages up, difficulty in assimilating new information and learning, and inability to cope up with stress that the environment could present are just some of the few reasons why brain training should be given attention at the earliest time possible.

Of course, you should have realistic expectations about brain training effectiveness if you want to try it for "super learning" needs. According to researchers, there are some conditions that would dictate its effectiveness. These are as follows:

- Training should be focused on brain functions that have measurable and practical real-life applications.
- Training should be aimed on perfecting the balance of functions.
- There is a minimum number of hours (15 hrs.) that should be allocated on training for a specific set of skill. Going below this minimum number will yield less desirable results.
- Training must be needs-based and not generic in design.
- Training must be consistently done. Plans should be created even before sessions are held.

Brain training is important most especially for those who are aiming to acquire "super learning" capabilities. The human brain is a complex learning tool which has a mysterious nature that is now being unraveled through continuous research. Its most controversial capability, neuroplasticity, will be discussed on the next chapter of this book.

Chapter 7: Using Brain Plasticity For Learning

Neuroplasticity or brain plasticity is the ability of the brain to change itself for the duration of the life of an individual. Yes, your brain is plastic! However, it is not "plastic" in the sense that it is made of actual non-biodegradable materials, but in terms of flexibility. There are connections in the brain that can be connected and rewired in many ways. The more connections are made, the better learning takes place.

Now, brain plasticity is manifested not only in learning, but also in many circumstances. These include the following:

- At birth to the early years of an individual where the immature brain is constantly developing.
- Situations where the brain has been subjected to physical injury. It tries to repair itself or increase the activity of some of its parts to compensate for the temporary loss of some essential cognitive and motor functions.
- Any instance wherein something new is experienced and deemed relevant to be remembered by the brain.

Going back to the link between learning and plasticity, there are principles that may have practical uses. You are reading this book because you want to increase your capability to learn, right? Understanding how plasticity works in the most basic manner will lead you to formulate your own courses of action towards improved learning.

The concept here is really simple. As you learn things, your brain undergoes chemical, physical and functional changes. The neural connections between cells in your brain get formed, rewired or grouped together depending on the strength of the stimulus.

The brain of humans is really designed to respond to stimulus and to adapt to challenges. It also has the functional capability to collate, interpret and act on information that comes in from the environment. The brain is an ever-evolving part of the body, which doesn't cease to function at certain age brackets, as what old neurological theorists are saying.

It is easy to see that the brain is like a muscle that must be kept active in order to be in good shape. The rule "use it or forever lose it" applies to this organ. Therefore, if we will use brain plasticity principles for our need to learn fast and with high efficiency, the clues are basically staring us in the face.

Let us now go to the ways through which you can apply plasticity principles to your learning needs. The first and most basic thing to do is to establish a daily learning routine that focuses on a single skill. Yes, it should be about one skill at a time. It could be about building the vocabulary or solving chemical equation problems. It is crucial to allocate only a maximum of 20 to 30 minutes for each learning or training session. The sessions could include small sub-tasks that are allocated about 5-7 minutes of time limit. Go beyond this and the plasticity effect on learning gets reduced.

After the routine gets established, one should make sure that the aspect of consistency is maintained. There is no such thing as cramming or rolling over the activities missed into another session. This is the logic behind keeping training or learning sessions short. 5-10 short sessions (30 minutes each) that are completed daily will have better learning benefits than a single session that lasts for a full 5 hours.

The last thing to do is to constantly increase the difficulty level of the tasks at hand. This way, the brain will try to keep up by building new neural connections or strengthening those that already exist. Difficulty levels should be increased slowly. It ensures that frustration levels will not build up on your part as a learner and hinder or lose the progress already made

Currently, there are online programs, courses and mobile device apps that claim to be designed based on the principles of brain plasticity. There is nothing wrong in trying out some of those things. However, you should be careful about outrageous claims like "instant results", "overnight improvement", or "know it all capability" coming from sources of these things. You're now aware of how plasticity works and this should guide you on making right decisions.

Chapter 8: Daily Learning Routines

Any learning system benefits from repetition and drills. Have you noticed that you have better chances of remembering something if you have seen it at least 3 times? Task outcome is affected by the level of concentration that we put on it. Concentration is something that we can do better if we have established a routine. Training the mind to do tasks at regular intervals of time makes it accustomed to the conditions of learning. When we get used to these learning tasks, our minds "crave" it naturally. Thus, learning becomes effortless for us to do under a routine-bound environment.

To simplify things, let us put it this way: when we create routines, we also create study habits. Of course, we will discuss some of these routines or habits that you should develop and follow for super learning purposes. Consider the following things that you should do:

- Plan your learning routines by allocating short periods of time for each study session. It is good to equally distribute learning tasks into several sessions instead of cramming it all up in one or two study periods.
- Assign a specific time of the day wherein you could study regularly and will not be disturbed. The worst mistake that you can make is to study only when there are random vacant times within the day. You must remember that solid routines support super learning outcomes.
- Accomplish relaxation activities before you start the learning session. This depends on your preference. Listening to music (classical) a few minutes before a study session has proven to be effective in boosting the cognitive functions of the human brain. If this isn't your style, you can just sit down and prepare your brain through a "quiet moment" before the learning task.
- Clarify the goals that you have for the study session. This puts a direction on your efforts. Write it on a piece of paper and stick it in an area where you can easily see it while on

the study session. Do this every time you study and you'll see how effective your learning capabilities are turning out to be.

- If you have several subjects or topics to cover, start out with the most difficult one. Follow it up with easier topics or tasks. This is a way to make sure that frustration levels will never hinder the completion of the learning or study session for the day.

- If you are doing an assignment, browse through your notes quickly first. This will jog your memory a bit and ensure that you will easily be able to relate previous learning with the assignment on hand. Looking back at the previous learning that you have accomplished is a great way to prepare your brain for more cognitive activities.

- Determine the right time to study with group mates. Usually, group studies are effective when there is no need to learn new concepts or lessons. Pure review tasks can be best accomplished if you are within a group. However, it is best to study alone when you need to learn something new from a material.

- Keep track of your progress for the day. Do you remember the piece of paper you have posted nearby? Look at it and see if you have accomplished the goals that are written on it. Accomplishing those goals give an individual a sense of satisfaction which further reinforces any additional learning acquired for the day.

Daily learning routines need not be too fancy or complicated. Just aim for consistency, simplicity and relevance to needs when you are planning and doing those routines. It would be good too if you can add the element of fun to it. Now that we have covered about the aspect of daily routines, we shall move on to the application of your learning. You can now proceed to the next chapter for more information.

Chapter 9: Learning Application

Surely, you are familiar with the line "learning by doing". Those who are in the education sector apply this when they use experiential learning techniques in the classroom. Apparently, the best way to solidify a learned concept or skill is to put it in action. This way, additional learning can take place and an individual can have an affirmation that he or she really has learned what needs to be learned. Again, this is connected to plasticity concepts. The more that learned skills are used, the more it will be retained within an individual.

In the super learning system, application is equated to an evaluation of outcomes. It is necessary that this part is planned too. In the planning process, you have to consider some very important things. One is about the level of thinking that is required for the application activities that you will accomplish. You must see to it that your way of thinking and using the previously learned knowledge or skill is valid. For example, you cannot measure level of memory by solving worded mathematical problems. It is also good to include room for combination of skills and concepts.

The next thing to consider is the complexity of the task that you will do. It is better to apply what you have learned on simple activities first. The level of difficulty can be adjusted on subsequent tries or application sessions. When a task has been accomplished, self-feedbacks or assessments can be done. Honestly evaluate your performance and ask if previous learning has helped with the kind of outcomes achieved.

When are you supposed to apply your learning? Experts in education and human development research will agree that application activities should be accomplished during and after learning sessions. Yes, during a learning session, you can immediately try to apply what you have acquired. This is a technique applied by teachers who immediately give seatwork or drills after presenting a lesson. Learning application after a study session strengthens results and progress made. Teachers give assignments related to the lesson that a class has just finished because they know about the principle we are discussing above.

Current researches on human brain and learning capabilities have revealed that repetitive application of skills and knowledge benefits the neuro-transmitting capability of the brain. Yes, this is responsible for memory and capability to process information quickly.

There are two ways through which you can carry out application of learning. One is through simulation of situations on which learned items are relevant. For example, you can simulate an emergency on which you need to remember the exact steps of an evacuation procedure. The accurate simulation of situation elements will add up to the strengthening of learned concepts and skills that will be applied.

Another way to apply learning is on real situations. The need to do this will depend upon the type of concept or skill to be applied. Have you ever tried to fix your non-functional remote controlled car after reading through its user manual? By presenting yourself with real-life scenarios for the application of what you have learned, a challenge is also created. Overcoming such a challenge is the biggest affirmation that learning goals have been achieved.

Super learning systems will always come with the need to apply concepts and skills acquired. You must be prepared to always test yourself and gain control over your speed of learning.

Chapter 10: Commitment To Life Long Learning

Most probably, you will think that when you finally graduate from college, your needs for learning will also stop. Of course, this is a notion that is always opposed by many education experts. The truth is that as long as you are alive, the process of learning continues. This is what we refer to as lifelong learning. The topics, concepts, methods, tips, and techniques of fast learning presented on this book don't exclusively apply in the classroom or academic setting. Yes, it extends out to the life that we have outside of school.

Your whole life itself is a never-ending source of learning opportunities. For every day that you wake up, go to different places, and meet people, you constantly assimilate in and process information. There is no such thing as the brain stopping on its functions when an individual finishes formal schooling. As long as the brain is active and you are alive, you will always be learning.

Of course, there are many interesting reasons to be committed to lifelong learning. These are as follows:

- ***Lifelong learners become big earners***: Current job markets evolve quickly these days. Every three years, skill set requirements for jobs could change rapidly. Those who learned multiple skills will have better chances of getting more than one source of income.
- ***Lifelong learners become people magnets***: This means that they become more interesting and are easy to get along with. They are good conversationalists because they know a lot and can share these depending on the topic at hand.
- ***Lifelong learners develop solid leadership skills***: Because you are interacting with lots of people, you learn from them fast and develop the skill to lead them. By constantly learning throughout life, you'll have an arsenal of solutions to a wide variety of problems and challenges.

- ***Lifelong learners gain the benefit of being independent***: Even if interacting with others is a requirement for healthy living, there are times when there is a need to do things alone. Lifelong learning allows an individual to gain skills which will be handy for their day to day living needs. Imagine being able to do all the repairs in your home without the need to hire a handyman. This is convenient and advantageous for you.
- ***Lifelong learners are able to maintain a good level of brain health***: The previous chapters have mentioned the importance of keeping the brain active through continued use. The more that you use your brain for learning, your tendency to become forgetful and stressed will be lessened.
- ***Lifelong learners gain better sense of satisfaction from life***: According to experts, there are three needs that humans need to fulfill in order to become really satisfied in life. These include purpose, a sense of mastery, and independence. Lifelong learning gives way easily to the fulfillment of these psychological needs.

You must realize from this point on that your commitment to lifelong learning is really important. Now that you have finished this book, you are armed with the knowledge, skills, and tools to learn fast. Use it wisely and continuously all the way through your life!

Conclusion

Thank you again for purchasing this book on ultimate learning!

I am extremely excited to pass this information along to you, and I am so happy that you now have read and can hopefully implement these strategies going forward.

I hope this book was able to help you understand the things you need in order to learn fast and how to apply learned concepts and skills in real life situations.

The next step is to get started using this information and to hopefully live a fulfilled, independent, and satisfying life!

Please don't be someone who just reads this information and doesn't apply it, the strategies in this book will only benefit you if you use them!

If you know of anyone else that could benefit from the information presented here please inform them of this book.

Finally, if you enjoyed this book and feel it has added value to your life in any way, please take the time to share your thoughts and post a review on Amazon. It'd be greatly appreciated!

Thank you and good luck!

Preview Of:

Ultimate Speed Reading Techniques!

<u>Speed Reading</u>

Begin Learning To Read 300% Faster In Less Than 6 Hours And Boost Productivity!

Introduction

I want to thank you and congratulate you for purchasing the book, Ultimate Speed-reading Techniques! Speed-reading Begin Learning To Read 300% Faster In Less Than 6 Hours And Boost Productivity!

This "Speed-reading" book contains proven steps and strategies on how to read content at a fast pace to keep up with the demands of work and life in general. It also highlights the need to improve reading comprehension while engaging in speed-reading.

Thanks again for purchasing this book, I hope you enjoy it!

Chapter 1 – Into The World Of Speed-reading

Reading brings our eyes, mouth, brain, and ears to life; it stimulates these vital senses. It also enhances brainpower along the way.

To Speed-read Is to See

In reading, everything starts by visually deciphering the words on the page, but how do you exactly look at the words when you read? Back then, researchers were convinced that humans read one single word at a time. They believed that we move our eyes across the page from the left edge to the right, digesting one word after another. This wholly explains how readers have no trouble identifying words at a faster than normal rate.

In reality, everyone (except those who are just starting to learn how to read) has the ability to read more and at a faster rate. As we weave through the page, we usually jump into fits and starts, reading a word (or a couple of them) in quick glances. It is in these quick glances stand the foundation of speed-reading. You know this as you go about reading several words in just a single glance, except of course when you encounter words that you are unfamiliar with. You also expand your vision unconsciously in an attempt to read and understand multiple words in a single glance.

To Speed-read Is to Read Silently

While reading, you tend to speak the words to yourself because you are used to reading them via the "sound-it-out" concept. Back at school, your teacher always told you to read words by sounding the letters and their combinations. Having that ability to sound out the words is an important skill for every beginning reader.

This approach slows you down however. You now read as fast as you would talk (we call this vocalization) and not at the speed of which you think, and there's a big difference. Saying the words, even whispering them inside your mind may take time, but that is how you speed-read.

Speed-reading Is Also Comprehending

People read because they want to comprehend what they read.

How well they comprehend what they're reading depends not only on their reading speed, but also on their vocabulary and familiarity with the subject matter.

Speed-reading generally increases your reading comprehension. Since you read multiple words at one time, you gain the ability to comprehend the words' meaning in context. It improves your general knowledge and vocabulary, and in turn increases your reading speed as well.

...and Concentrating

Reading requires concentration, but if you engage in speed-reading, you must display forceful and sustained concentration – you do many things at the same time while at it. Effective speed-reading means you must be able to read down the words while remaining alert to what the article/book's author wishes to impart to you, especially understanding how the material is presented so you can fully comprehend the main ideas at the same time. Once this is achieved you begin to read fast with a better perspective.

Thanks for Previewing My Exciting Book Entitled:

"Speed Reading: Ultimate Speed Reading Techniques! Begin Learning To Read 300% Faster In Less Than 6 Hours And Boost Productivity!"

To purchase this book, simply go to the Amazon Kindle store and simply search:

"SPEED READING"

Then just scroll down until you see my book. You will know it is mine because you will see my name "Ryan Cooper" underneath the title.

Alternatively, you can visit my author page on Amazon to see this book and other work I have done. Thanks so much, and please don't forget your free bonuses

DON'T LEAVE YET! - CHECK OUT YOUR FREE BONUSES BELOW!

Free Bonus Offer 1: Get Free Access To The OperationAwesomeLife.com VIP Newsletter!

Free Bonus Offer 2: Get A Free Download Of My Friends Amazing Book "Passive Income" First Chapter!

Free Bonus Offer 3: Get A Free Email Series On Making Money Online When You Join Newsletter!

GET ALL 3 FREE

Once you enter your email address you will immediately get free access to this awesome **VIP NEWSLETTER!**

For a limited time, if you join for free right now, you will also get free access to the first chapter of the awesome book "**PASSIVE INCOME**"!

And, last but definitely not least, if you join the newsletter right now, you also will get a free 10 part email series on **10 SUCCESS SECRETS OF MAKING MONEY ONLINE!**

To claim all 3 of your FREE BONUSES just click below!

Just Go Here for all 3 VIP bonuses!

OperationAwesomeLife.com